St Budeaux

Yesterday's Village

Marshall Ware

Two local ladies are here collecting their meat for the week from Mr. C. Robertshaw, then the only butcher for the area working from nearby Ford. This scene is in Edith Street, the year is 1892 and the day is either a Tuesday or a Friday as these were the delivery days for St. Budeaux. Note the state of the road and the two curious young onlookers.

This version of the book is virtually as originally published, presenting the work of Marshall Ware. There are now additional pages at the back providing information about the publisher, Arthur L Clamp.

The republishing project is being managed by Arthur's grandson, Steven Gibson. We aim to find all the research that he was involved in publishing, preserving it for the next generation as part of 'The Clamp Collection'.

ST. BUDEAUX: YESTERDAY'S VILLAGE

I am dedicating this booklet to Dr. J. Emrys Owen, who has looked after our welfare for over twenty-nine years and Miss Anne Slemon, who was born at Bull Point on the 25th October, 1882. They think that many of the photographs taken over 60 years ago with my box camera, of the houses and farms which have disappeared, should be recorded for posterity. This has been made possible by Arthur Clamp, who has planned the reproduction of the pictorial records for publication.

I have lived in Saltash Passage for over seventy years and two of my friends, Wilf Doble and Chris Stoneman. still live in houses built before 1831 and Mr. and Mrs. W. Binding have just celebrated their diamond wedding anniversary.

I have seen St. Budeaux grow from an almost self-contained village where most of the chapel people voted Liberal and church people voted Tory, to an urban community. We had limited transport, so everyone had to walk and so recognised each other. I think Leslie Hore-Belisha was our favourite M.P. because he took such an interest in all our local organisations. I remember the early days of the Labour party and the election cries of "Ham and eggs for all" and "We are all brothers now".

Our councillors, James Ware (1872-1930), Station Ward, and George Daymond, Tamerton Ward, played a large part in the local social life. My father was a member of the newly formed Rifle Club and was treasurer of the Horse Show and Regatta Committee, and Councillor G. Daymond was the treasurer and provided a hut for the Y.M.C.A.

My interest in local history started in 1910, when I first met Mr. H. Montagu Evans (1842-1930) who gave me one of his greenstone neolithic axes which were discovered below Ernesettle Wood; axes of a similar nature were found in the nineteen sixties on the Brown and Sharpe factory site. In 1898, when the militia were doing their summer training at Ernesettle Fort, Capt. Mullins and Mr. Evans found a granite trough, thought to be a Saxon font, which was taken on a gun carriage to the Garrison Church at Crownhill. When the Army Church was demolished, the font was taken to St. Aiden's Church, Ernesettle, and rededicated by the Bishop of Plymouth. I was an executor of the Evans Estate and inherited his papers *St. Budeaux: Its Manors and First Church*, copies of which can be seen in the local library.

Our history starts in the year AD 480, when the Breton Abbot, *Budoc*, came to Tamerton Creek and introduced Christianity to St. Budeaux. He erected a crude stone cross in Ernesettle Wood, to serve as a baptistery for his flock and formed a sanctuary field near Warren Point, near where the first chapelry was built. He founded a Monastery on the Isle of Lavret just off the coast of Brittany and died there in AD 500. Mr. Evans was the honorary curator of the Devonport Museum from 1890 to 1914 and will be remembered for his transcript of the parish registers which date back to 1538 and recorded the location of Drakes Hill on the old St. Budeaux map. He discovered the marriage entries of Henry Newman's five children:-

1552 Nov. 25th Lyon Worthie and Maude Newman.
                (Lyon Worthie was Lord of the Manor of East Whitleigh)
1560 April 29th John Bodman and Margaret Newman.
1565 Aug. 19th Robert and Johan Newman.
1569 July 4th   Francis Drake and Mary Newman.
1571 Sept. 4th Mr. John Sanders and Elinor Newman and the death of Lady Mary Drake.
1582 Jan. 25th Mary Drake, wife of Sir Francis Drake.

No trace of Lady Mary Drake's tomb or grave has been found. None was known in 1863, so it cannot have been among those obliterated by a concrete floor laid during the restoration of St. Budeaux Church in 1876. He also found the Norman Tympanum, now in St. Budeaux Churchyard, thought to be part of the first church, which existed up to 1482.

It is not generally known that the Cornish Patch or Little Ayshe Barton, St. Budeaux, in the Manor of Trematon, consisting of 120 acres was in the Duchy of Cornwall, forming part of the ecclesiastical parish of St. Stephens, Saltash, up to 1895, when it was transferred by a local Government Board Order No. 32169 dated 1st April, 1895, to the civil parish of St. Budeaux.

Our local public houses have a very interesting history, particularly the *Royal Albert Bridge Inn*. The earliest known reference is contained in a Manor of Trematon copyhold deed, dated 6th November, 1822, when John King, Richard King and James King, customary manor tenants, sold *Dock Inn*, orchard and garden to Francis James (Victualler) for £295. In 1823 the name was changed to *Devonport Inn*, and to the *Royal Albert Bridge Inn* in 1860. Bradford Leslie (later to become Sir Bradford Leslie), one of Brunel's engineers, resided in the Inn and in 1855 married the landlord's daughter, Mary Jane Elizabeth Honey. I hope to deposit a full history of the inns in the local library this autumn.

My article on the history of Budshead Mill and Mount Edgcumbe Training Ship have been published in the Western Morning News; the articles on the Little Ash Tea Gardens and Deacon's Blacksmith's Shop were published in the Western Evening Herald, copies of which will also be deposited in the local library this autumn.

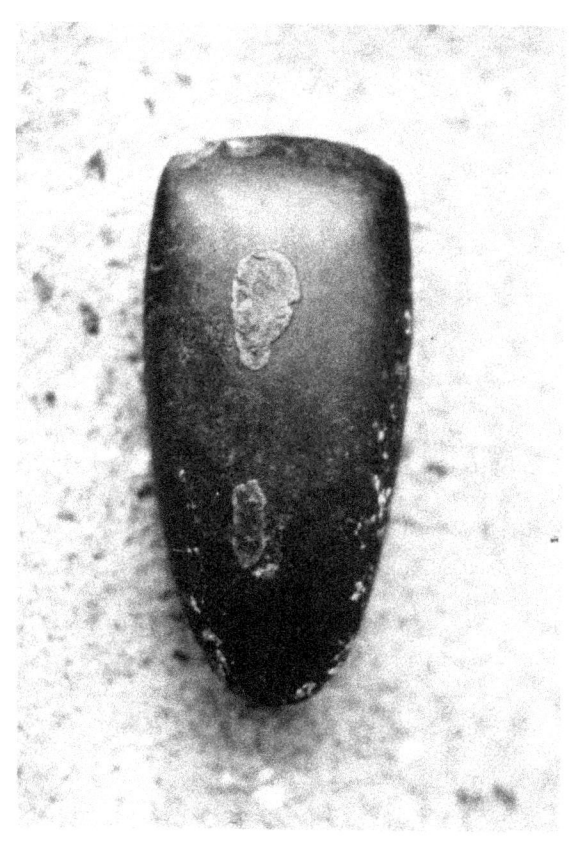

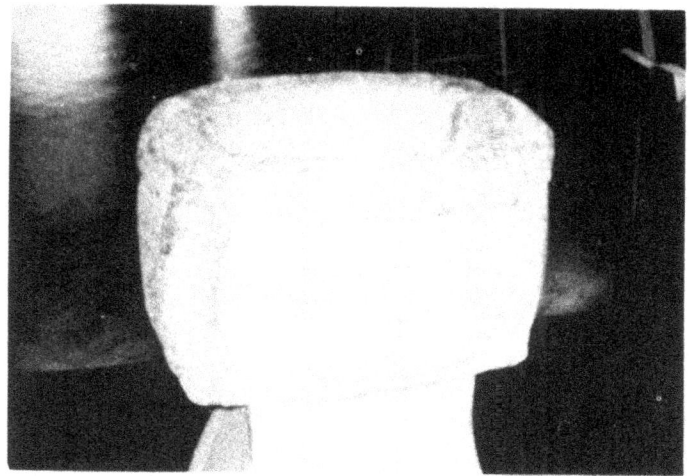

SOME VERY EARLY REMAINS

The neolithic greenstone axe pictured on the left was one of several excavated below Ernesettle Wood in 1898 by Captain Mullins and a team of militia men. Similar stones were also found during the 1960s on the Brown and Sharpe factory site indicating what must probably be the site of the first or one of the earliest settlements in this locality. The fine Saxon font now in St. Ardens Church was discovered by H. Montague Evans in 1898 and taken to the Garrison Church at Crownhill by Captain Mullins.

The large granite stone below is possibly a relic of the earliest church at St. Budeaux. It is a roughly semi-circular tympanum having on its face a cross recessed within a circle. It originally stood in front of Agaton Farm and was taken by the Rev. Parkinson to its present position in St. Budeaux churchyard.

These Devon and Cornwall boundary stones situated below the Cornwall Gate Inn mark the eastern boundary of the "Cornish Patch", part of the Manor of Trematon, which was in Devon from 1329 to 1898. Unfortunately most of the incised lettering on the stones has worn away.

To the left is the Very Rev. J. T. Trelawny Ross who gave the site for St. Boniface Church in 1900. The Trelawny family were the main local landowners going back to 1639. Above is a portrait of Field Marshall the Right Hon. Viscount Wolseley after whom the former main road leading from Plymouth to Saltash was named. This was opened on 15th July, 1836, and replaced the road via Weston Mill. Lord Wolseley of Cairo was a friend of Colonel John Chard of *Rorke's Drift* fame and stayed at his home at Mount Tamar.

The photograph of Mount Tamar, taken in 1910, was formerly the seat of Captain Sir Thomas Byard, R.N., who is buried in St. Budeaux churchyard where there is a monument to his memory. John Chard lived there in 1849, who won the V.C. in 1879 for the defence of *Rorke's Drift* during the Zulu war. The house was taken over for an Open Air School for delicate children on the 1st November, 1920, and Miss Anderson was the first head teacher. On each remembrance day she made laurel wreaths from garden shrubs and placed one on the Byard Memorial in the church and the other over John Chard's photograph as illustrated. The mansion was demolished in 1974; their names are perpetuated by Chard Road and Byard Close.

SALTASH PASSAGE AND THE RAIL BRIDGE

This waterside view was taken in 1890 showing horses waiting to haul up the muddy beach a laden cart. This was a common occurrence for many years with extra horses waiting to assist carts and carriages after leaving the small ferry boat. Note the onlookers.

This framed view of Saltash Passage and Brunel's bridge dates from the 1880s. The ferry can be seen on the far side of the water, the *Mount Edgcumbe* training ship just beyond the bridge and, in the foreground, Taylor's stables overshadowed by the trees.

This old picture postcard shows the start of the Saltash Passage residential development in Higher Quarry Park, Higher Kiln Park and Lower Kiln Park, all then in St. Budeaux in the County of Cornwall. The field to the right was part of Little Ash Farm of 65 acres and 2 roods let to Thomas Tozer in 1858 for £115 per annum.

The water from Weston Mill Lake ran past Barn Quay, Weston Mill Quay (now known as Camel's Head Quay), Lob Quay, right up to Weston Mill village. This old wooden bridge was known as "Shaky Bridge" or "The Switch Back" because it was all ups and downs. The state of the bridge was discussed at the St. Budeaux Parish Council meeting on the 11th November, 1897, because the twelve inch holes were a danger to foot and vehicular traffic. An embankment was built in its place across the creek which enabled the Devonport and District Tramway Company to provide "a through service" from Devonport to Saltash Passage in place of the Camel's Head shuttle service which started on 26th June, 1901.

THE TRELAWNYS

This sign used to hang outside the Trelawny Hotel and depicts the family coat of arms with the latin inscription *Sermoni Consona Facta* which translated reads "May your deeds match your words". The seal of General John Jago Trelawny can be seen on a conveyance for the sale of part of Barne Estate in 1895 for £265 on the right.

Miss Murril Searle of St. Budeaux lent me this photograph taken on 10th June, 1919. H.R.H. The Prince of Wales has just received a cup of tea and a piece of saffron cake and is seen talking to her grandfather, Mr. J. P. Kerslake, who at that time was the oldest employee on the Duchy Estate. The demobbed army man has just received a small holding by the Prince on very generous terms.

One of the bygone pursuits of many local people years ago was rabbit hunting with dogs and ferrets. This 1898 photograph shows such a group about to set out on a day's hunt accompanied by one person in military uniform, probably from a local camp.

This 1895 photograph of a St. Budeaux Parish councillor with the traditional bowler hat was taken on one of the footpaths to illustrate the typical slip bar and swing gate provided for pedestrians. Protests were made when Government authorities removed many in the area. The last stile, swing gate and a granite slip bar remained on Little Ash farm until 1920.

The ferry in 1912, the charge for crossing then being 1d. However, if anyone was late the boatman would row the person across for 2d. using the small boats in the foreground. To the north can be seen part of the old horse boat ferry, *Mount Edgcumbe* training ship and H.M.S. *Implacable*.

Most of the nonconformist, chapel people voted Liberal and thought the Church of England was State aided. They supported the 1914 Bill, to be raised in Parliament for the dis-establishment of the Church of England and the abolition of tithes. Only a small portion of the latter went to the local vicar and the rest was sent to Mr. Whitford of St. Columb who held the "tithe rent charge". The St. Budeaux Parish protest against the Bill was led by the vicar, Rev. Watson, followed by Messrs. Brown, Bradford, George Cole, the headmaster of the C. of E. School, Mr. Warring, with wife and daughter, Ellie, under the banner. The man with the board was Mr. H. Montagu Evans (1842–1930). As a Liberal candidate, the popular Mayor Leslie Hore-Belisha, in 1922, defeated Sir Clement Kinloch-Cooke, the Conservative M.P. for Devonport. This is one of the few St. Budeaux photographs shown of him, presenting a valuable silver bowl to Mr. George Thomas, chairman of the local sailing club. 8

Do you remember the privately owned shops in Yeoman's Terrace and our beloved St. Budeaux Square prior to the Tamar Bridge works? The ancient elm tree, planted by General Trelawny, dominates the scene of this part of St. Budeaux.

St. Budeaux Foundation School in this photograph will be the most recent building to disappear from this area. What would the senior governor and churchwarden, the late W. E. Baker of Agaton Farm think? His son, Fred, has been a governor for over 50 years and approves of the new school in Priestley Avenue. The charge to attend the now closed school was once 2d. per week.

St. Budeaux Charity school, built on Agaton Green, dates back to 1717. A Rev. T. Alcock raised the money to provide "a salary of £18 for a schoolmaster and to provide clothes for as many poor children as the charity would permit". The school was transferred to the present site in 1867.

YESTERDAY'S SHOPS IN THE VILLAGE

On the 1st October, 1895, the Plymouth Co-operative Society purchased Stuart House in Trelawny Road for £900 and converted it into a grocery and butchery shop at a cost of £339.

In 1901 Tom Occleshaw converted his Yeoman Terrace residence into a hairdressing and tobacconist shop lit by oil lamps and was later the first shop to have gas lighting. His son, Sidney, continued the business concentrating on the sale of sweets and tobacco. On his death Robin ran the business but sold out in October, 1980, to another firm. The locals were sorry when the name Occleshaw disappeared from the scene. Other shops were opened by Mr. Truscott, a respected Baptist, who started a boot makers business and the Menheneotts opened a dairy. Mr. Blackmore sold cream and butter from 1 Yeomans Terrace and Mr. Eastlake had a general shop. A Ford butcher, Mr. Robertshaw, sold meat from his van on Tuesdays and Saturdays.

It opened on 1st December, 1895, with Mr. W. Shepherd as manager followed in 1901 by Mr. A. D. Hammett. He had two assistants and one apprentice who was paid twelve shillings for a sixty hour week. The staff are assembled wearing their aprons for this photograph.

St. Budeaux Church where Francis Drake was married was built in 1563. The oil lamps illuminate the stained glass windows, erected by W. E. Elliot of Ernesettle in memory of his wife who died in 1860. The Sir Ferinando Gorges memorial tomb can be seen behind the organ.

The Rev. B. J. S. Vallack with his wife, four daughters and one son, as seen in 1870 outside the imposing entrance to the vicarage described on the old deed as "contiguous to the churchyard and within the sanctuary". In 1827 it was a mere cottage containing only two rooms on the ground floor. After his appointment in 1832 he spent a large sum of money to enlarge the building as a thanksgiving for the "removal of cholera from these parts".

The Rev. W. L. Green was appointed in 1886 and lived in the new vicarage (now the Cornwall Gate inn) after the old vicarage fell into disrepair. He went everywhere in his "buggy" pulled by his shetland pony. He was not liked by the parishioners because on the 10th February, 1898, the parish clerk was instructed to write to the County Council for them to take action to compel the vicar and the churchwardens to hand over to the parish council the tithe map, documents and books. He was replaced as chairman by C. P. Prance (Barne Towers).

The Budshead Mill was fitted with three pairs of stones for grinding wheat, barley and oats and was built by John Gonk in 1791 for George Leach, the owner of the farm, who rented the mill and the tidal basin of over 6 acres to him for a nominal consideration for the first three years. Subsequent owners were Richard Hall Clark, of Pennycross, in 1798, followed by Lord Ashburton in 1840, and Earl Compton, his kinsman, succeeded him. His tenants were Walter King (1805-1869) followed by William King (1832-1912) and William Davey in 1887. He was succeeded by his son, the popular Harold Doney, who vacated the Mill and Farm in 1924. The older Mill for the modernised farm ran up to 1802 and the cottages were occupied by the long serving members of the Ide family.

This very faded photograph shows Mrs. B. Petherick standing in front of the overshot wheel of Weston Mill. Mr. Petherick, engineer and wheelwright, made carts, wheelbarrows, etc. In 1155 the land was owned by Godrey de Weston.

St. Budeaux Open Air School for delicate children was opened at Mount Tamar on the 1st November, 1920, by Lady Astor. Miss Elizabeth Anderson was the first head teacher, who left in 1930 to take charge of a similar school in Liverpool. On each Remembrance Day, 11th November, she made laurel wreaths from the garden shrubs and placed one on Captain Byard's Memorial in St. Budeaux Church and another on the photograph of Lieut. John Chard, V.C.

Royal Navy camp at St Budeaux as it was in 1925. Following the First World War it was decided to build a shore based camp H.M.S. *Vivid* in order to train cooks, stokers, writers and supply hands. It was dubbed by the locals as "White City". The picture gives an excellent view of the fields and open land which once surrounded the village. Now almost all of it has been developed for residential purposes.

This group photograph of personnel at the camp includes Cyril Pearce, in the back row, who lives in Pemros Road opposite the old site. The uniformed sailors were a once popular sight in St. Budeaux, providing colour and trade for the local shops.

Moor Farm gets its name from the adjoining ancient highway with that name and in 1680 was owned by William Treville. Prior to 1883 it was owned by Mr. Ryall who owned a brewery as well. The brewery horses were kept at the farm, which in those days extended almost to Camel's Head creek. The first tenant in 1883 was George Wakeham Proctor, followed by John Proctor in 1900, when it was owned by W. F. Stuttaford, passing to Irving Stuttaford about 1914. It was farmed by the Proctor family until 1935, when the land was sold to Plymouth Corporation. The farm house and buildings were demolished to make way for the new Council estates. The ancient Manor Farm, King's Tamerton, below, was owned by the Trelawnys of Ham, Weston Mill. The last line of tenants for over forty years were William Cole and his son, George Cole. The farm land was acquired by the Plymouth Corporation in 1935 and the farm was demolished for the Council estates.

The upper picture is a general view of Barne Farm, consisting of 168 acres, with new developments in the background of which Sithney Street and Colrenick Street are parts. General J. G. Trelawny inherited the estate in 1883. In the 1530s the farm was in the hands of the Beele family, the last male heir marrying about 1674 to the daughter of Jonathan Trelawny of Coldrenick, Menheniot. The Avent family were farmer tenants for many years, the last being Joseph who retired in 1870, then followed by the Cuddefords, about 1883 to 1916, and lastly by William Luscombe who sold it to the Plymouth Corporation. Lower Ernesettle Farm was named after William Ernstell, a freeholder of Budshead in 1428. The farm is dated 1653, but stands on the site of a previous farm. It was farmed for many years by members of the Cocks family who were connected with the Three Towns Dairy in Westwell Street, Plymouth, where delicious cream teas could be obtained. The farm has been demolished for a car park.

WESLEYAN METHODIST CHAPELS

The above shows Higher Ernesettle estate chapel built in 1893 upon a site given by Mr. Newby Spooner. It is now used by the local branch of the British Legion. The Meeting Chapel below, Millbrook Cottage, was registered in 1858 by Thomas Knight, superintendent shipwright of H.M. Dockyard. Knackersnowle (Honicknowle) Wesleyan Chapel, to the right, was built in 1812 and demolished when the road was widened.

LOCAL CHILDREN AT VICTORIA ROAD SCHOOL

Can anyone recognise themselves in these photographs? On the left can be seen Miss Anne Slemon with her class sometime during 1905. She is still in St. Budeaux and is now the eldest resident of the area. She was born at Bull Point on 25th October, 1882, and went to the Government School in 1886.

When the Bull Point school closed in 1896 the boys went to the Masonic Hall and Edgar Phipps, from Ford, took charge. The girls went to the Wesleyan Chapel with Miss Baily in charge. The children were transferred to Victoria Road School in 1902 with Mr. E. Phipps as headmaster and Mr. Olden was the caretaker.

Children from the St. Budeaux families of Daymond, Hooppell, Camp, Dyer, Cole, Short, Doidge, Martin, Truscott, Foster, Peard, Haymam, Boon, Tolley, Rowe, West, Hammett and Dustan attended. Among those included in Mr. Norman Bucknell's class are Dennis, Anstis, H. N. Bucknell, Gilbert, Foster, Harrison, Jones, Ellis, Winter, Cruze, Morgan and Knapman.

VICTORIA ROAD SCHOOL STAFF

Back row: Miss L. Packer, E. Petherick, H. N. Bucknell, T. Garland, L. Williams. *Front row:* Miss D. Teppett, Miss Little, N. Phipps (headmaster), Miss I. Worth, Miss H. Woods and Miss Fuller. Boys and girls received an excellent education from these dedicated and respected teachers.

This group of local people assembled for the opening of the new rifle range at St. Budeaux in 1913. Seated in the front row are N. Bucknell (schoolmaster, Victoria Road school), Mrs. Thomas, wife of Dr. T. J. P. Thomas and Tom Occleshaw, the local barber.

One of St. Budeaux's local football teams: Kinterbury Villa seen here in 1923 when they won the Junior League Cup. J. Reid, then inside right, is still living in St. Budeaux. The club was disbanded in 1924. Bob Foster, who played inside left joined Saltash Stars and later played for Cornwall and Reuben Woolway, goal-keeper, joined Looe football club.

Awaiting the arrival of a train at the London and South West Railway station, St. Budeaux. The station master was then E. Tolley who had a staff of two seen in this illustration. Many local people travelled to work in Plymouth from here each day.

This goods train was derailed on the 12th September, 1892, on the broad gauge Cornwall Railway single line, just below the St. Budeaux (Ferry Road) station which was opened on 1st June, 1904. The driver was killed and sabotage was suspected. Note the first eight houses of Morris Park Terrace and the ancient elm tree which remained there until about 1928.

Another once common scene in this area was this two-coach motor train running to Millbay Station in Plymouth. The fare from St. Budeaux was 3d. per return! Note the driver holding a staff to regulate the single line working over the river bridge. The picture dates from 26th August, 1906. These early multiple coaches are still in use but now in the form of diesel units.

ROYAL ALBERT BRIDGE AND ITS INN

This quite unusual and somewhat dramatic view of the interior of the rail bridge was taken sometime during 1906. It gives a very good view of the complex ironwork required to hold the bridge together.

The Royal Albert inn was formerly the Dock inn in 1822 but when Plymouth Dock had its name changed to Devonport in 1824 the inn followed likewise in title. It changed its name again in 1860 after the completion of the rail bridge. It was a convenient coaching inn for the nearby Saltash Ferry traffic and in the census of 1841 eleven people resided here. J. W. Stoneman became the tenant landlord after the inn was acquired by the Octagon Brewery, followed by his son, Robert, who returned from South Africa to take over. The cottage was incorporated in the premises by the subsequent owners, Courage, and is now one of the attractions of the waterside.

During the First World War it was constantly patrolled for security reasons, a task undertaken by troops from the East Surrey Regiment stationed at Wearde Camp, Saltash. A sergeant Selley was responsible for the safe guarding of the bridge.

This was a familiar scene from mid-April until September at Saltash Passage showing the start of the Royal Albert Bridge Sailing club "handicap boats" competing for the Harkcom Cup. All the boats were locally owned as membership was confined to residents of Saltash and St. Budeaux with about equal membership from both sides of the Tamar. The first President was General T. C. Porter of Trematon Castle.

This view shows the slipway approach to the quay to provide an access to Wolseley Road for the use of ferry passengers under the ancient "Passage of Saltash Ferry Rights". The steamship, S.S. *Saxon*, is unloading a cargo of 650 tons of coal which was discharged by twelve stevedores on this occasion in 1910. Ships were loaded at Goole on the Monday to arrive at Quay on Thursday.

The Saltash ferry is seen here beached for repairs sometime in 1908. Note the stable and the flag on the Ferry House Inn then owned by the Borough of Saltash. The original house was built in 1575 and converted into a coaching inn during 1850 which was said to be haunted.

SOME ROAD AND BOUNDARY STONES

The two upper illustrations show unusual local boundary stones. The left had a letter "T" cut into it which referred to the Rev. Trelawny of Ham and E. Trelawny of Coldrenick, both prominent landowners. The one on the right was at the corner of Peter's Park Lane and shows that it was part of the old highway maintained by the Saltash Turnpike Trust and indicating the distance to Saltash Passage. This stone is exactly matched by another at Burraton, Saltash. The St. Budeaux stone has disappeared with road widening work.

The stone below was erected following the extension of the Devonport boundaries in 1898 when it took in 940 acres of St. Budeaux land. It is below the Royal Albert Bridge and can still be seen with its legible lettering. The round stone is situated two miles from Plymouth opposite Camel's Head public house. Note at its base the Ordnance survey bench mark. The three mile stone just beyond St. Budeaux Square on Ferry road has disappeared. Wolseley Road by the Turnpike Act of 1823 superseded the old Saltash Road as the highway into Cornwall.

The stone laying ceremony for the new St. Boniface Church took place on the 4th November, 1911, on a site given by the Rev. Dr. Trelawny Ross of Ham. The church was consecrated by the Bishop of Exeter on the 14th May, 1913, supported by N. Watson, vicar of St. Budeaux Church.

A Roman Catholic place of worship was needed for the inhabitants of this locality so on the 3rd October, 1933, Father James Symons from Devonport registered three rooms on the ground floor of the Presbytery, Pemros Road. It continued in use until the 14th February, 1934, when the new church, St. Paul's, was built and opened.

St. Peter's Mission Chapel built during 1885 to serve the needs of the growing numbers of new people to this area. It was dedicated to the memory of a local resident, Admiral Sir Peter Richards, K.C.B., Lord Commissioner of the Admiralty. Unfortunately it was destroyed by enemy action in April, 1941, and not rebuilt.

The Rev. Burgin was very proud of his 1908 choir supported on his left by Mr. Warring, headmaster of the Foundation school, George Cole, organist on his right, Mr. Rawlings, assistant manager to Mr. Warring. He is next to Miss Congdon at the back. Also to be seen are George Bradford, Percy Dollery and James F. Donne.

The prominent position of St. Budeaux Church dominates the local scene providing beautiful views of the river Tamar and numerous Cornish parishes.

The picture below shows the old Crownhill road to the left of which stands the church, its vicarage behind and the partly hidden St. Budeaux Inn, now the Blue Monkey. On 16th August, 1644, the Royalists made use of the church and churchyard as a garrison and were defeated by the Roundheads. Several cannon balls were discovered in the hedges when the road was widened in 1910.

THE VILLAGE IN THE 1890s

The delightful early photograph above is dated the 8th July, 1899, showing the laying of the memorial foundation stone for the Queen Victoria Masonic Hall. The early Lodge meetings were held in the Trelawny Hotel on the invitation of General J. J. Trelawny. In the foreground is Mr. Gimblet, the local postmaster, with pony and trap.

To the right is the last of the old Millbrook Cottages which stood until 1899 when it was demolished to make way for the then new Victoria Road, named after the Queen. One was occupied by a Mr. Moyle who worked on the construction of the Royal Albert Bridge.

This notice appeared in 1846 for Millbrook Cottages. "Millbrook Cottages near King's Tamerton. To be let from Michaelmas next. Four new cottages consisting of three rooms each and a garden. Rent £5 per annum. A portion of land will be let with each cottage if required."

25

HORSE POWER IN ST. BUDEAUX

The old St. Budeaux Horse Show was a very popular annual event and received widespread support from local farmers and tradesmen. Entries were received for all classes from places as far apart as Liskeard and Totnes. First class judges coming from away were given accommodation at the Trelawny Hotel and General Stone (Mount Tamar) was the chairman from 1910 onwards. Mr. R. Luscombe of Warleigh, Tamerton, was a well known breeder of horses and won many of the prizes. On the 9th July, 1894, Mr. M. E. Tripp acquired from the Duchy of Cornwall three roods of the "Water of Tamar, parcel of territory possessions of the Duchy of Cornwall". James Tripp built the quay in 1898 with stone from Little Ash quarry. It was taken over by James Ware who changed its name and used it until 1922. Mr. Ware poses with his teamsters as they prepare for the day's work. From left to right is Fred Cole, James Ware, Fred Johns, Jack Baker Brown and Jim Friend. Mr. Whiteford, driver of Cuddeford's milk float stands outside the Barne Lane toll gate. The Cleave family were local carriers and kept their powerful horses on Camel's Head Quay. They had Naval and Dockyard contracts and carried much local building material.

We have to thank H. Montague Evans (1842-1930) for the large number of photographs he took of Budshead. The ancient manor house, built soon after the Norman Conquest, was pulled down about 1808 and rebuilt in 1810. It was converted into a farmhouse but is now a ruin. The picture gives a good impression of the stone gateway which formed the main entrance from the lane.

This was the second vicarage, in Vicarage Road, acquired before 1886. Francis Rundle bought the property from the Ecclesiastical Commissioners in 1958 then it passed into the ownership of H. and G. Simmonds (now Courage) and was converted into a modern inn, the present *Cornwall Gate*.

The photograph of the Stuart building "Ham", substantially built of granite and limestone, was taken before 1912. It sustained enemy attack during the last war and part of the east wing was destroyed. It appears to have been built in 1639 by Robert Trelawny who was a staunch Royalist. It ceased to be a private residence after the death of the Rev. J. T. Trelawny Ross, D.D., in 1935. After that date most of the Trelawny property in the area was sold to the Plymouth Corporation.

SHIPS ON THE TAMAR

The *Mount Edgcumbe* training ship seen here flying its flag was once a well known ship moored just north of the rail bridge from 1877 to 1920. Originally she was the 50 gun H.M.S. *Winchester*, and in her later life was converted to training young boys for the sea. At one time there were 250 aboard her, they had a band and a full staff.

In 1922 the Admiralty sold a number of unwanted Tamar based destroyers to Marple and Gillott of Sheffield for scrap iron. This included H.M.S. *Acorn* seen here which is being broken up at Ware's Quay. In the background is Baden Terrace, St. Peter's Church and Godolphin Villas.

The river Tamar was the principal way of bringing in or taking out of the area stone, produce, materials, etc. until the construction of the main roads. This view of the *Shamrock* coastal boat dates from 1926 and shows her on one of her last trips entering the river Lynher to collect "stone ballast". She was one of dozens of craft working in the local waters. Fortunately she has been saved and restored and can now be seen at Cotehele Quay.

All the St. Budeaux babies were delivered in the home by local midwives and Granny Uren who was well respected for her caring work. Even Dr. Smith, the first local doctor, left this duty to her. She is seen here with daughter, grand-daughter and great grand-daughter.

LOCAL PEOPLE

All set for a good day's outing from the Trelawny Hotel. This photograph shows one of the annual outings of the St. Budeaux Working Men's Club some occupying the high open seats of the coach. The hotel was built by Major General John Jago Trelawny, owner of Barne estate, in about 1895. The first landlord was Joseph Striplin, followed by Harry Hearn.

This is Barne Towers, home of Cecil P. Prance who was chairman of St. Budeaux Parish Council in 1894. The Cornwall boundary stone stood in the western hedge. Unfortunately the house was destroyed by enemy action in 1941 and its site is now occupied by a garage filling station.

In 1860 W. E. Elliot built an embankment and reclaimed 120 acres of the Tamar mud flats and built this picturesque building, "Newlands", on the nearby land. At the turn of the century it was bought by the *Mount Edgcumbe* training ship trustees for a sick bay and cottage hospital. It was given by the trustees to Captain Harkcom, in lieu of a pension, and was compulsorily acquired by the Ministry of Defence to make an entrance to Ernesettle Depot.

The cart is an example of Edward Petherick's (Weston Mill) workmanship which helped Fred Cole with the gentle giant *Boxer* to win the blue rosette at the St. Budeaux Horse Show in 1912. The station yard has gone to make way for a car park and Yeomans Terrace is now the shopping centre. During the First World War goods trains delivered large shell cases to the yard for filling with explosives. In 1915 1,309 tons and 4,052 tons in 1916 were carried and from then onwards A. Currin and W. Cleave (Camel's Head) helped the transport with their horses.

DEACON'S BLACKSMITH SHOP

This was built on the old Saltash Road running from Plymouth to Saltash ferry and met an almost daily need for repairing broken carts and carriages and shoeing horses. In 1878 James Deacon was the blacksmith and postmaster. Letters were sorted at Devonport and carried by a donkey to the adjoining Traveller's Rest, which was the home of the Deacon family. He was succeeded by his son Charlie Deacon.

The old tram lines can be seen in the lower picture at Donne's Corner, Saltash Passage, so named after James Donne who built the house (The Firs) and Lynher Park House soon after 1871. Charles Trelawny of Coldrenick explored the lead-silver deposits here in about 1837. The adit runs under the road and the old mine building in Little Ash Quarry

ST. BUDEAUX CUP

This very valuable St. Budeaux cup is dated 1534 and inscribed "The gift of Johanna Andrews, St. Budeaux, 1708." It is on permanent loan to the Plymouth City museum for exhibition.

As part of the peace celebrations following the ending of the First World War all the children living at St. Budeaux were given cups on the 4th August, 1919. They were handed over by Lady Sir C. Kinloch-Cooke on the playing field. They were made at Torquay and, as there are so few left, have become collector's items.

On the 6th February, 1900, the Baptists opened a mission in a room above a stable belonging to Mr. Henwood (Baker) at the rear of Yeomans Terrace. It was registered by Leonard Smith of Devonport. This room was superseded by the building shown here which opened on the 16th February; 1902, and built by Tozer and Allen, registered by Henry Smart, 2 Lynher Terrace, St. Budeaux. This old building in Wolseley Road is now used as a garage.

The illustration showing the marquee and flags is of Little Ash Tea Gardens visited by over 20,000 people a year and owned by the Plymouth and Devonport Tramways Company. A once very popular beauty spot and a treat area.

In 1898 the Borough of Devonport extended its boundaries by taking 940 acres from St. Budeaux Parish (then in Plympton R.D.C.) and created two new Wards, *Tamerton* and *Station*. My father, James Ware (1872-1930), was elected resident councillor for Station Ward. In the 1912 election there were 457 electors. The results were:

Ware (Conservative)	185
Cook (Labour)	69
Sanders (Independent)	31
Bayley (Ratepayers)	25 Total: 210

Lieut-Commander E. W. Rogers represented St. Budeaux Ward for many years and served as Plymouth's Lord Mayor during 1934-35. He had a distinguished career in the Royal Navy (Torpedo Branch) and was a Methodist Church Sunday School teacher.

One of the earliest views of the building expansion into this area after the new L. and S.W. railway station was opened in 1890. Note the ancient elm tree, station house and toll gate, bottom of main Barne Road, before Victoria Road was built.

Royal Albert Bridge Sailing Club (now Tamar River Club). Cups presented by the Commodore. These were donated by General T. C. Porter and Miss Jaen Porter (Trematon Castle), Leslie Hore-Belisha (M.P.), Captain H. Wesley Harcourt (Mount Edgcumbe Training ship) and C. Magner (Royal Oak, Cargreen). Mr. L. Alexander was chairman and Mr. M. Ware treasurer.

This very unusual tomb is that of St. Budoc who died in AD 500. He had returned to Brittany and established a Foundation on the Isle of Lavret off the coast following his missionary work in the country.

ACKNOWLEDGEMENTS

The author wishes to express his thanks to the following people who have either loaned photographs and gave permission for their use in this title and to many others who in one way or another have offered information and given advice on the history of St. Budeaux.

Fred Carter, our village postman born in 1892 (his uncle Jim Carter built the Masonic Hall), Mrs. Edginton, E. Tripp, Chris Stoneman, Mrs. Violet Waldren, Miss Ethel Procter, Mrs. E. Dawson, Wilf Doble, G. Selley, Mrs. Robert Foster, Bert Collins, Mrs. Bertha Lambie, Mrs. Roy Oliver, Fred Cole, Mrs. I. Gray, Philip John, Joe Currie, and last but not least, members of the Hooppell, Hammett and Donnie families. To Arthur L. Clamp for making the production of this title possible.

This booklet is dedicated to the not too distant years gone when St. Budeaux was a village and to the people of those days who contributed to its everyday life and character.

Arthur L. Clamp – the man behind the books

Arthur Leslie Clamp was a man of boundless energy with a passion for helping others, particularly through his love of history. A printer by trade, he started his career in a printing company before moving his family from Exeter to Plymouth to teach at the Plymouth College of Art and Design, where he eventually became the Head of the Printing Department.

A Devoted Family Man

Despite his love of teaching, Arthur prioritised his family, always making it home by 5:30pm for tea. He and his wife, Rosemary, raised five children: Susan, Angela, Elizabeth, David, and Steven. Arthur would often combine his love of family and history by taking his children on Sunday walks, encouraging them to appreciate historical monuments by taking photos or making crayon rubbings of gravestones for his books. The family home at 203 Elburton Road was a hub of activity, with a large garden, featuring a two-storey fort and a makeshift swimming pool.

Arthur with his five children.

A Lifelong Learner and Adventurer

Arthur's thirst for knowledge extended beyond history to a deep curiosity about the world. He was passionate about exploring different cultures, traditions, and cuisines, often taking advantage of his long summer holidays as a teacher to travel to places like India, Russia, South America, the middle east and the USA, sometimes bringing one of his children along. This adventurous spirit even influenced his home life, as seen by the short-lived family tradition of steam-cooking vegetables after a trip to Iceland.

History is a prominent feature of family days out

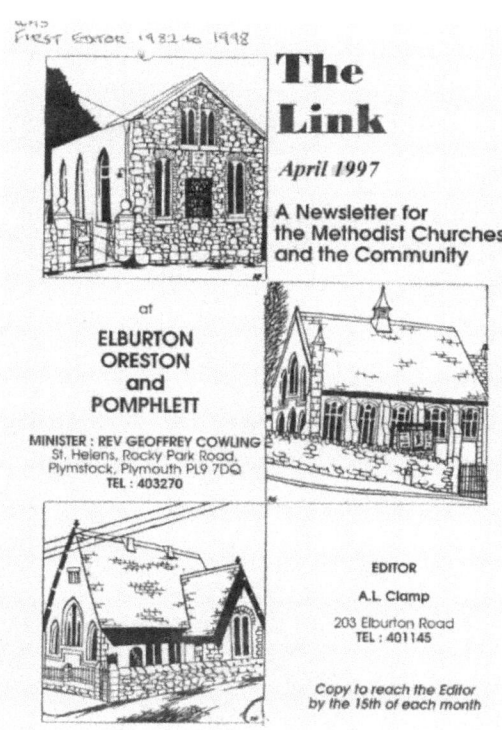

Community and Philanthropic Spirit

His commitment to serving others was evident in his long-standing involvement with the Elburton Methodist Church. He was the Sunday School Superintendent for over 15 years and served as the editor of the wider church's monthly newsletter, "The Link," for a similar duration. After Rosemary's very sad passing, Arthur later remarried and, following a chance encounter with a professor from India, established a connection with a missionary school in Chennai. Together with his new wife, Christine, he co-founded a "Sponsor a Child's Education" program that continues to this day.

*Pictured left – The cover of 'The Link' complete
with hand drawn sketches of each church by Angela
Below right – Arthur Clamp promoting his latest book
Below left – Arthur at home with his first wife, Rosemary
Below centre – Arthur on holiday with his second wife,
Christine*

A Legacy of Learning and Positivity

Arthur's greatest passion was history, which he brought to life through tireless research, documentation, and the many books he authored. He was driven by a need to "never be stuck in a rut," constantly seeking new experiences, meeting new people, and expanding his knowledge. With a positive attitude and a great sense of humour, he was always ready to help others, leaving a lasting impact on his family and community. His children, Susan, Angela, Elizabeth, David, and Steven, remember him with love and gratitude.

David Clamp, 2025

A Legacy of Local History

Below is the story of how Arthur L Clamp began writing books, in his own words, drafted shortly before he passed away in 2001. I have only made minor alterations to this text, correcting grammatical errors that he did not survive to correct himself. When I first discovered this text, I was shocked to see my name mentioned. It seems that, unbeknownst to me, I shared my first PC with him. I suspect he used it during the day when I was at school, although I do have one memory of sitting with him and showing him how it worked. It has been a pleasure to pick up where he left off and see his books republished and redistributed, and to know that I was part of the story, even back then. It was also fascinating to discover that his pricing structure matches the way I have tried to price the books, with a third going to local sellers and the rest covering printing costs with a little left over for my expenses.

I am his eldest grandson, and it is a privilege to curate his legacy, which we are calling 'The Clamp Collection'. The very last line of the text originally reads "The following pages list all the titles." Sadly, that page is missing and we have no record of all the books he published and knowing that some of those were researched by other authors makes the process of finding them even harder. I look forward to one day completing the collection and seeing them all available again. And maybe, one day, I'll even start writing my own to add to the series. For now, here is his story in his own words.

Steven Gibson, 2025

Writing and Publishing Booklets on Local Topics and Areas

I started this interest in either 1968 or 1969 when living in Woodford. I had by these dates established the Department of Printing and I think I must have been looking for something different to do. The first titles were of A5 size proofed from type set at Clarke, Doble and Brendon, Ltd., Plymouth printers, and then made up into pages and printed at Sawtell and Neilson, Ltd., Totnes.

Then began a slow process of getting them out to shops, etc. which proved to be more time consuming and difficult than actually researching, writing and getting the books into print. However, I persisted and opened a business account with Barclays Bank on the Broadway. I was advised to give it a title so I called it "Westway Publications". There came along another problem, one of storage of paper and finished books which was solved when the family moved to Elburton in 1970.

I changed the printer to Penwell, Ltd., Callington, Cornwall, as he was then just setting up himself and his prices seemed very reasonable. I did not get any of the printers to make up the complete books. I hand folded the flat printed sheets, stitched the books on a small manual table stitcher and trimmed them in a small hand turned guillotine which I bought from someone in Penzance for £40. It was brought up in a van.

The trouble and time going to and fro to Callington was too much so I transferred the printing to PDS Printers, Prince Rock, Plymouth, and I have been with them ever since. Now they are at Plympton which is easy to reach and they fold the flat sheets which was turning out to be a long chore which only saved a small part of the printing costs.

All my first titles were written by myself. I took the photographs and developed them in the loft of the house, the type was set by now on a computer situated in the house at Elburton from which I had collected photographic lengths of text to cut up and law down as pages.

At some point I decided that I would do my own film processing of lith film so I bought a large second hand process camera from Kingsbridge and learnt through trial and error to make line negatives of the text and halftone negatives of the illustrations which proved more difficult than I anticipated. The main problem was trying to keep the developer in the large dish at the correct temperature as any change would affect the developing time. I replaced this old camera with a brand new one bought from Croydon, Surrey, costing £900. This has turned out to be a great asset cutting out an expensive part of the printer's costs and one crucial aspect of the work which I could control.

By the middle 1970s there were many outlets I had contacted in Plymouth, up to Dartmoor, Exeter, around to Torbay, Totnes, Dartmouth and the South Hams. The market for local books was much greater than I had first thought and through getting to know many local people undertaking research themselves had the chance to help and make up books for other people who had in most instances, got together a collection of photographs with some text in a rather muddled way. Through my experience in print I was able to shape up their work and get it into print and in every case I had to pay the printer and let the person have the royalties. In the majority of titles produced in this manner this was another way of producing titles and it did give some profit to my work. However, I must say that in a few cases I lost out by either the other person getting the numbers wrong, not returning any monies from stock I delivered or they thought that more of their books should have been sold.

The print run was usually 1,000 copies and from time to time I have had reprints of 250 copies. It took about ten years to clear the first print run so I always had large stocks in the garage, workshop, etc. The numbers sold during the early years was about 7,000 copies a year increasing to around 9,000 copies and for the whole of the enterprise about 500,000 have been sold. The booklets have become part of the local scene and many people collect them, shops regularly order copies and I go around certain areas month by month restocking or replacing titles as necessary.

During the past year or so I have started setting the text on a Packard Bell PC, something which I should have done some years back. I share it with Steven Gibson, my grandson. There appears to be no end to the market for local books, but I could not earn a regular income because of the long time it takes to sell stock.

However, now exceeding 100 titles made up mainly of A4 twenty-four page booklets, some folded guides, with selling prices set with a third going to the shop which is the trade custom, the original idea has been quite successful and could go on for ever.

Apart from monetary benefits, however spasmodically these might be, I have learnt a lot myself, met many interesting people and have become part of the local scene with requests to give talks and to advise people about getting into print.

Arthur L Clamp, 2001

This newspaper article, published by the Evening Herald on 17th August 2001, forms a good record of his life. Just as he encourages us to learn more about local history, we encourage you to learn a little about him. For that reason, we have included these pages at the back of all the most recently republished books, in honour of his memory and recognition of his contribution to the community.